MAGIC MOMENTS

Edited By Andy Porter

First published in Great Britain in 2022 by:

Young Writers
Remus House
Coltsfoot Drive
Peterborough
PE2 9BF
Telephone: 01733 890066
Website: www.youngwriters.co.uk

All Rights Reserved
Book Design by Ashley Janson
© Copyright Contributors 1970
Softback ISBN 978-1-83928-634-6

Printed and bound in the UK by BookPrintingUK
Website: www.bookprintinguk.com
YB0MA0005G

FOREWORD

For Young Writers' latest competition This Is Me, we asked primary school pupils to look inside themselves, to think about what makes them unique, and then write a poem about it! They rose to the challenge magnificently and the result is this fantastic collection of poems in a variety of poetic styles.

Here at Young Writers our aim is to encourage creativity in children and to inspire a love of the written word, so it's great to get such an amazing response, with some absolutely fantastic poems. It's important for children to focus on and celebrate themselves and this competition allowed them to write freely and honestly, celebrating what makes them great, expressing their hopes and fears, or simply writing about their favourite things. This Is Me gave them the power of words. The result is a collection of inspirational and moving poems that also showcase their creativity and writing ability.

I'd like to congratulate all the young poets in this anthology, I hope this inspires them to continue with their creative writing.

CONTENTS

Alderman Jacobs Primary School, Whittlesey

Eva Jackson Neale (10)	1
Hibbi Richardson (11)	2
Marianka Borowicz (10)	3
Sienna Mawby (10)	4
Pearl Okogwa (9)	6
Sophia Cox (10)	7
India Meen Ward (10)	8
Elly McCoy (8)	9
James Busby (9)	10
Alyssa Woodward (8)	11
Imaani Campbell (10)	12
Jessica Pycroft-Gibb (10)	13
Rose Rowden (10)	14
Meredith Overend (9)	15

Ashford Park Primary School, Ashford

Mayra Majumdar (9)	16
Gracie Wigley (9)	17

Ballymagee Primary School, Bangor

Cassie Craigen (11)	18
Tom Posner (11)	19

Beardall Fields Primary And Nursery School, Hucknall

Lennox Xavier (8)	20
Charlie T (7)	21
Billy Boffy (8)	22

Berkeley Primary School, Berkeley

Daniel Fishpool (9)	23

Brooke CE (VC) Primary School, Brooke

Jessica Bailey (7)	24

Castleford Park Junior Academy, Castleford

Ella Pashley (11)	25
Skyy Nuuns (9)	26
Jacob Wilson (9)	28
Logan Mason (10)	29
Grace Hutt (9)	30
Riley Harvey (11)	31
Emily Berry (8)	32
Kayden Greenwood (10)	33
Summer Hughes (10)	34
George Lalley (11)	35
Dawid Kulig (10)	36
Laiton Orr (9)	37
Ellia Rowlands (8)	38
Ozzie Butterfield (10)	39
Emily Butler (10)	40
Rosie Brown (11)	41
Keira Grace Leadeham (11)	42
Nicole Sherwood (11)	43
Louis Addy (11)	44

Chessington School, Chessington

Lucas Preda (12)	45
Chloe Watson (12)	46

Ty Alleyne (13)	47
Tristan Padberg (13)	48

Collingwood School, Wallington

Kim Do (11)	49

Coton-In-The-Elms CE Primary School, Coton-In-The-Elms

Dylan Anderson (11)	50
Kaden-Jaye Bell (10)	51

Easington Colliery Primary School, Easington Colliery

Jack Storey (11)	52
Mia Lawler (11)	54
Amelia Veitch (11)	55
Luke Mathwin (10)	56
Kieran Mcgloen (11)	57

Elms Farm Primary School, Birmingham

Mayson Griffin (8)	58
Samir Mohammad (8)	59

Featherstone Primary School, Erdington

Keiva Bailey (10)	60
Inayah Sheraz (11)	62

Harvington CE First School, Harvington

Archer Blaxall-Kimber (9)	63
Edward Dorrell (9)	64
Emilie Zidani (9)	65
Harrison Black (8)	66
Bobby Callins (8)	67
Heidi Bishop (10)	68

Henry Green Primary School, Dagenham

Ummi Hoque (10)	69

Leicester Islamic Academy, Leicester

Muhammed Bukera (10)	70
Aaminah Bukera (9)	71
Ayana Shakeel (9)	72
Awaab Hassan (10)	73
Shahir Salman (9)	74

Leuchars Primary School, Leuchars

Samantha Lorimer (7)	75

Loretto Junior School, Musselburgh

Honor Porter Davison	76
Stella Jenkins	77
Ellie Evans (11)	78
Alice Lockie (11)	80
Xavier Jandrell	81
Oscar Borthwick (10)	82
Sofia Legorburu (11)	83

Lower Kersal Community Primary School, Salford

Jasmine Leah Robinson (10)	84
Alicia Grace Robinson (10)	85
Dario Ludwig (8)	86

Maplesden Noakes School, Great Buckland

Gabe Simmonds (12)	87

Milton Abbot School, Tavistock

Nevaeh (10)	89

Nailsworth CE Primary School, Nailsworth

Luca Dulare (10)	90

Newtonmore Primary School, Newtonmore

Charlotte Harper (8)	91

Normanhurst School, North Chingford

Enis Hacimusa (8)	92

Our Lady & St Peter RC Primary School, Bridlington

Aidan Blades (8)	93
Nikodem Biernat (9)	94
Josh Miller (8)	96
Nico Ferre (9)	98
Jayson Celohorty (8)	99

Our Lady of Perpetual Succour Primary School, Widnes

Freddy Derbyshire (9)	100

Phoenix St Peter Academy, Lowestoft

Lily Woolmer	101
Imogen Rose Lapping	102
Ellie Felton (7)	103
Hadleigh Hitcham (9)	104
Lacie Lapping (9)	105
Dempsey Dyer (8)	106
Kenzy Hoskin (9)	107
Ronald Stanaitis (9)	108
Evie Grist (10)	109
Alexis-Grace Woolmer-Crosswell (9)	110

Saints & Scholars Integrated Primary School, Armagh

Darcy Orr (10)	111
Tyler White (9)	112

South Rise Primary School, London

Shushil Varsani (10)	113
Justin Rwatangabo (10)	114

St Anthony's Primary School, Spateston

Ella Whitehorn (11)	115

St Mary's Catholic Primary School, Tilbury

Sam Falusi (11)	116
Alexandros Mistakidis (11)	118
Fiyin Osinuga (11)	120
Samuel Onafuye (9)	121
Sophia Chimereanyinma Ogu (9)	122
Tilly Fagbore (9)	123
Lisa Addo-Tenkorang (9)	124
Ellie Beadle (11)	125
Amarachi Oguledo (11)	126

St Mary's CE (VC) Primary School, Bridport

Miriam Digy (10)	127

St Mary's RC Primary School, Clapham

Marsela Martini (10)	128
Thomas Mushrafi (10)	130
Zachary Harper-Simpson (11)	131
Jayden Gyamfi-Robinson (10)	132
Megan Cadavid Monuz (10)	133
Triomphe Peres (11)	134
Tyrone Kwaako (11)	135

Stefan Fernandes (11)   136

St Stephen's CE Primary School, Little Harwood

Hawwa Zabar (8)   137

The King's School, Macclesfield

Darcie Morris (10)	138
Max Westwood (10)	140
Sef Cooper (11)	141
Ariyan Nassab (10)	142
William Wallace (8)	143
Jack Hutchins (11)	144
Ella Collins-Webb (11)	145
William Johnson (10)	146
Charlie Kay (11)	147
Freddie Robinson-Pickles (8)	148

The Shade Primary School, Soham

Ava Stephenson-Hyde   149

The Thomas Coram CE School, Berkhamsted

Charlie Mardon   150

Tweedmouth Community Middle School, Spittal

Taparni Delamere (11)	151
Sadie Gregory (11)	152
Isla Stewart (10)	154
Layton Reap (10)	155

Wakefield Methodist Junior & Infant School, Thornes

Grace Emma Howson (8)	156
Bella Reid (9)	157
Betsy Reid (9)	158

Wallsend Jubilee Primary School, Wallsend

Belle Downey (10)   159

Westgarth Primary School, Marske-By-Sea

Olivia Carroll (7)   160

Westlea Primary School, Westlea

Liam David (10)	161
Libby Matter (11)	162
Kerem (10)	163
Oliver Gardner (11)	164
Elissia Doka (10)	165
Shawn Rodrigues (10)	166

Wildridings Primary School, Netherton

Jackson Hall (8)	167
Grace Townsend (7)	168
Xiyuan Ju (8)	169
Matas Gecevicius (8)	170

Windmill Hill Academy, Windmill Hill

Phoebe Hinks (10)   171

THE POEMS

This Is Me!

This is me and I love my family,
My name is Eva just because I'm a diva,
I'm gonna blow you away with my supersonic sway,
I like eating pizza just because I'm a diva,
In my heart I am tall but in real life I'm small,
I like doing hip hop as well as TikTok,
I like eating gum and my fingers are always numb,
I hate wearing masks but at school I'm really good at tasks,
I love to do gym as well as swim,
I like to eat chocolate treats as well as dance to the beats,
I love to draw as well as sip out straws,
I also love to sleep as well as dig deep,
I always turn on the light and stare up at the stars at night,
So this is me, I love my family, I have lots of energy so you can't judge me.

Eva Jackson Neale (10)
Alderman Jacobs Primary School, Whittlesey

My Grandma, The Robin

When it's winter I see you fly,
As I look up to the vast, blue sky.
I see you soaring in the frosty breeze,
And are very glad you do not freeze.

When I spot you in your comfy nest,
I look at your glimmering eyes and crimson breast.
Your chocolate coating melts in the sun,
And your sapphire rhombus chirps when you are having fun.

My ears are filled with your sweet tune,
In the morning, in the evening and at noon.
You and your new friends sing songs together,
Even in the worst of weather.

You once were my grandma in human form,
But when you let go I dare not moan.
Now I realise you can fly with glee,
So go with your sisters and brothers and fly free.

Hibbi Richardson (11)
Alderman Jacobs Primary School, Whittlesey

I Am Me

I am me, you see,
And me I want to be.
I like my hair, my face, my shoes,
My smile and clothes, it's not big news!

I love my family and my friends
(Not always, I cannot pretend.)
I like my teachers in my school,
All of them are really cool.

Look, I know a lot of you out there,
Look in the mirror and say: "It's not fair!"
You think you're ugly, fat and plain,
Your life is terrible and terrible it will remain.
If you think that, you are insane!
And that I won't repeat again.

You are not ugly, fat or plain,
Your life is not terrible, and that is how it will remain.

Marianka Borowicz (10)
Alderman Jacobs Primary School, Whittlesey

Not Quite Eleven

I have,
Green eyes through which
I've seen wonders of the world.
I have,
Keen ears to hear amazing
Sounds
All around.
I have,
Long legs, so I can run around
The world
Restlessly.
I have,
Hands with which I write,
Type,
Draw.
I have,
Arms to hug
And show affection.
I have,
The love of my family
Which spreads through me

Endlessly.
I have,
Friends who are always there
To laugh and sometimes share
A tear.
This is me,
I will never change
Because I will never be anyone
Else
And I am only ten!

Sienna Mawby (10)
Alderman Jacobs Primary School, Whittlesey

I'm Who I Want To Be

This is me, I'm who I want to be.
I've struggled to make friends but made enemies just by walking by.
Now I have two best friends who love me.
I have no regrets because this is me and I'm who I want to be.

I have an amazing family who,
Like my friends, love me no matter what.
We might fight but what family doesn't?
This is me and I'm who I want to be.

I'm unique and not like anyone else.
This is me and I am who I want to be.

Pearl Okogwa (9)
Alderman Jacobs Primary School, Whittlesey

You're In Your Spirit Form, But Still My Grandma

You dance on your paws,
In your spirit form,
You dance on the street,
Looking for something sweet,

The way you smile warms the day,
And makes the darkness go away,
The dog of you runs around the park,
As you make a gentle bark,

The day you passed it was hard,
But I knew you were in my heart,
You are at rest with Grandad,
I know that now you are not sad,
You're happy and starting a new adventure in your new form.

Sophia Cox (10)
Alderman Jacobs Primary School, Whittlesey

Be As Bright As A Shooting Star

Be as bright as a shooting star,
Be happy with who you are,
Be proud with what you have achieved,
Tackle obstacles that you come across,
Believe in your dreams,
Have a positive attitude to your learning,
Be polite to your teachers and be kind to your friends,
Have good manners and celebrate each other's differences,
Be gentle like a puppy,
But be brave like a lion,
Be happy with who you are,
Be as bright as a shooting star.

India Meen Ward (10)
Alderman Jacobs Primary School, Whittlesey

What To Be?

Ping-pong, football, badminton, boxing, makeup testing
Wondering what to do?
Watercolour painter, teacher, dress designer
So many things to do!
Dog groomer, vet, or a farmer
So many things to be you.
Actor, author, taxi driver, basketball player
So many things to do!
There are so many choices to what I could be,
And so many things I like.
So take a guess of what you think I want to be,
I wonder will you be right?

Elly McCoy (8)
Alderman Jacobs Primary School, Whittlesey

All About Me!

My name is James,
I like to play games,
I dream to be a machine maker,
For a Red Bull driver,
I come from Northern Ireland,
But I live in England now,
I like to play the piano,
People may think different about me,
But I think I am kind, funny and helpful,
Here are some things I say to you:
Be kind,
Treat others as yourself,
Express yourself,
Go over and above,
Finally, be yourself.

James Busby (9)
Alderman Jacobs Primary School, Whittlesey

Sister And Me

I play princess, sister holds my dress.
I point my toe, sister has a go.
I ride a bike, sister rides a trike.
I read a book, sister takes a look.
I play outside, sister wants to hide.
I like to draw, sister paints the floor.
I swim about, sister splashes out.
I rollerskate, sister hesitates.
I wave goodbye, sister starts to cry.
I'm home again, then sister's happy then.

Alyssa Woodward (8)
Alderman Jacobs Primary School, Whittlesey

The Real Me, Imaani

This is me, Imaani - I was born a twin destined to win.
Faith and hope I hold within.

I ntelligent
M ighty
A stonishingly
A pt
N oble
I n fact.

Verbose, not trying to boast. *Clink, clink,* let's toast.
To me, to us, in God we trust.
On the path to victory, come and share it with me... Imaani!

Imaani Campbell (10)
Alderman Jacobs Primary School, Whittlesey

All About Me

I am an adventurous kid,
I'm a chatterbox and I can't keep on the lid,
I don't like wearing a dress,
I like getting mucky and making a mess,

You'll find me where the animals are,
Or walking the dog when we go far,
You'll find me with a horse in a stable,
Or working on my artwork at the table.

Jessica Pycroft-Gibb (10)
Alderman Jacobs Primary School, Whittlesey

This Is Me, Rose!

I am a girl,
When little, I had a curl,
Long legs and tall,
Always on the ball,
My name is Rose,
And I like to pose,
Always on the move,
My feet constantly groove,
Singing, dancing, gymnastics,
Make me look fantastic.

Rose Rowden (10)
Alderman Jacobs Primary School, Whittlesey

Emotions

Sticks and stones
Can break my bones,
Why be like everyone else
When you can be yourself?

Roses are red
Violets are blue,
I was so sad
When I was with you.

Meredith Overend (9)
Alderman Jacobs Primary School, Whittlesey

Covid Caught Me!

The virus has caught me,
Can't you see?
I'm poorly and sick,
And as weak as a toothpick.
I lie in my room,
Feeling like I'm in a trap of gloom.
But I'll soon get better,
And Covid won't cover me like a sweater.

Mayra Majumdar (9)
Ashford Park Primary School, Ashford

Winnie

I got a dog and her name is Winnie,
And she's got the ears of a rabid bat.
She's not so fat.
Oh, we call her Woo Woo Ninie Lamborghini.
Little girl, puppy.
Oh, Woo Woo Ninie.
Oh, Woo Ninie.
Oh, baby puppy.

Gracie Wigley (9)
Ashford Park Primary School, Ashford

Doggo

D ogs are fluffy or silky soft, being hyper and hungry
O r calm, chill and not hungry at all.
G o to the park and play fetch.
G o to sleep my little doggo on your little bed
O r when asleep go on the sofa.

Cassie Craigen (11)
Ballymagee Primary School, Bangor

Summer's Day

A summer's day is one for play
Ice creams, lollies on a beach day
Water splash
Fun and laughs
Happy children.

Tom Posner (11)
Ballymagee Primary School, Bangor

This Is Me

I'm a pizza devourer
I have a lot of power
But pineapple makes me cower
I'm great at skateboarding
Good at video games
My feet go fast just like a flash
I play basketball and I'm not a cheetah
I like sweets, especially strawberry flavour
I'm a dreamer and a believer
Good at scoring and bad at ignoring
And I hate swimming
I mostly win by the skin on my chin
This is me so I can be who I want to be
And that's me, who I want to be
This is me.

Lennox Xavier (8)
Beardall Fields Primary And Nursery School, Hucknall

This Is Me

Legs as fast as a lion.
To win water races.
Mouth as big as my school badge
That eats McDonald's.
Arms as long as ladders
To play Lego and PS4.
Eyes as bright as the sun
To let me see in the dark.
This is me.

Charlie T (7)
Beardall Fields Primary And Nursery School, Hucknall

This Is Me!
A kennings poem

Game winner
Park player
Maths hater
Lunch eater
Trip lover
Chocolate chomper
Switch gamer
History expert
This is me.

Billy Boffy (8)
Beardall Fields Primary And Nursery School, Hucknall

This Is Me

T he name is Daniel.
H ave many skills.
I love football.
S kateboarding is fun.

I love jumping.
S ometimes I play with Owen.

M y favourite game is red light, green light.
E gypt is my favourite country.

Daniel Fishpool (9)
Berkeley Primary School, Berkeley

Jessica

J oyful Jessica is always happy
E xcited and ready to learn English
S ports are good for my body
S weets are what I love
I vy is my friend
C ecily's otters are
A dventurous.

Jessica Bailey (7)
Brooke CE (VC) Primary School, Brooke

I Love Being Me

My heart is a kindness river,
it flows but never stops.

And when that kindness river knows,
it puts a smile from hope to home.

I love when people smile,
it shows me today is going to be a happy day.

My family will guide me, light my way so bright,
and the words you hear me say are,
I love being me,
I know I may be quiet,
I know I may be happy.

But I will make my mark and show
the world my passion.

For I can make my little light come to life,
and let you see.

I am happy for being ME!

Ella Pashley (11)
Castleford Park Junior Academy, Castleford

How To Make Me

A pinch of happiness.
10ml of kindness.
A handful of helpfulness.
One tablespoon of love.
A bowlful of caring.
A pinch of braveness.
A tablespoon of resilience.

Pour in a bowl and stir until thick mixture.
Pour on a baking tray with baking paper.
Put in the oven for fifteen minutes.
Put a pinch of love and happiness on top of the cake.

How to make the toppings:
One tablespoon of sweetness.
Two pinches of independence.
20ml of kindness.
A bowl of caringness.

Put in a bowl and then in the fridge for five minutes.
Then pour it on the cake,
Add a pinch of kindness, love,
Braveness, smartness, happiness and caringness.

Skyy Nuuns (9)
Castleford Park Junior Academy, Castleford

How To Make A Demon

To create me you will need:
Blue eyes,
Blonde hair,
Pale skin,
A dash of blood,
Glasses.

Add 987 sticks of butter to the human features.
You will also need 789 roast dinners with drumsticks.
50 dashes of fiestiness and happiness,
100 dashes of spiciness,
One Nintendo Boomerang Fu game of life,
One million teddies

Now, add the human features, names,
Add the dashes of feelings, and the demon is made.

Jacob Wilson (9)
Castleford Park Junior Academy, Castleford

My Life

L ogan is my name, I'm as strong as Hulk Hogan.
O utrageously lazy is the reason I'm called crazy.
G one as quick as Flash, I'll dash around the world.
A s I hate Liverpool, they'll lose to any dual.
N o for Liverpool, they are not cool. If you support them then you are a crazy fool.

My dog's called Fifi. She is very beefy.
She'll watch TV and drink a cup of tea.

Logan Mason (10)
Castleford Park Junior Academy, Castleford

This Is All About Me

G ood at Fortnite.
R eally excellent at singing.
A nd great at dancing too.
C hocolate, my favourite Galaxy is the best.
E veryone says I'm a great help to my mum.

H appiest when I am colouring in.
U nhappy when things go wrong.
T ogether with my brother, I play.
T ill my dad says it's bedtime.

Grace Hutt (9)
Castleford Park Junior Academy, Castleford

I Can't Wait To Be Twelve

Things are always alright when I play Fortnite.
My cousin is a baby and she raps like Slim Shady.
Leeds United is my team, to meet Kalvin Philips is my dream.
I spend time with my friends, it makes me sad when it ends.
I play footie and love a chip butty.
I am swag and that's not a lie,
If I had a fight with KSI,
It's time for him to say bye-bye.

Riley Harvey (11)
Castleford Park Junior Academy, Castleford

This Is Me!

E asy to annoy.
M cDonald's is my favourite food.
I enjoy art and dance.
L oves shopping.
Y ouTube watcher.

B obby is my dog's name.
E ncanto is my favourite movie.
R oblox player.
R obux wanter.
Y ounger brother is very annoying.

Emily Berry (8)
Castleford Park Junior Academy, Castleford

I'm Different From Everyone

I love to see my new puppy
I love to hear my family talking
I like to touch my Oculus Quest 2
I like the smell of super noodles
I love the taste of chicken nuggets
I love to play football and my Oculus Quest 2
I am brave
I am smart
I am fun
I am friendly
I am fearless.

Kayden Greenwood (10)
Castleford Park Junior Academy, Castleford

Hello

Hello. I don't like yellow.
I live in Cas, I don't have sass.
I just walk and talk.
I like green, I'm not mean.
(At least, I don't think so.)
I don't like to feel low.
I like cats.
Soon I have my SATs.
I like a cup of tea.
I like to be me!

Summer Hughes (10)
Castleford Park Junior Academy, Castleford

My Life

I'm a Leeds fan through and through,
But I miss all their goals when I go to the loo,
And I also play footie,
But I can't resist a chip butty,
My dog's name is Flo,
Wait, I have school. I've got to go!

George Lalley (11)
Castleford Park Junior Academy, Castleford

I Am...

I am a gamer.
I am a good friend.
I am a family member.
I am a lion, strong and brave.
I am a Pokémon collector.
I am a football card collector.
I am a Spider-Man supporter.
This is me.

Dawid Kulig (10)
Castleford Park Junior Academy, Castleford

This Is Me

I am kind.
I am nice.
And also I love rice.
I love to draw.
I love to colour.
I love my family and the summer.
I am cool.
I am good.
I am funny.
And finally...
I have money.

Laiton Orr (9)
Castleford Park Junior Academy, Castleford

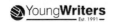

What Do I Like? This Is Me

A kennings poem

Art lover.
Family carer.
Doughnut muncher.
Ice pop licker.
September girl.
Animal lover.
Mum's little helper.
Stargazer.
Moon watcher.
Bird liker.

Ellia Rowlands (8)
Castleford Park Junior Academy, Castleford

Ozzie

I am Ozzie, I am always in the way.
When I'm in the way I never go away,
Look left, look right, doesn't matter which way.
My name is Ozzie, I'm always in the way.

Ozzie Butterfield (10)
Castleford Park Junior Academy, Castleford

This Is Me
A kennings poem

I am a...
Panda, koala, rat, ferret, hamster, and guinea pig lover.
Light sleeper,
Food eater,
Early riser,
Pasta chomper,
And finally,
A loyal friend.

Emily Butler (10)
Castleford Park Junior Academy, Castleford

All About Me

A kennings poem

I am a,
Football watcher,
Wasp fleer,
Football player,
Early waker,
Light sleeper,
And finally a Leeds United follower.

Rosie Brown (11)
Castleford Park Junior Academy, Castleford

All Me!

K ind as I can be,
E legant like a fairy,
I ndependent and lairy,
R eliable and free,
A mazing me.

Keira Grace Leadeham (11)
Castleford Park Junior Academy, Castleford

This Is Me

Drawing is my passion.
Friendships and walks are a must.
I'm made up of lots of little things,
And I am one you can trust.

Nicole Sherwood (11)
Castleford Park Junior Academy, Castleford

Louis

A kennings poem

I am an...
Inspirational rugby player
Funny person
Family lover
Animal person
Friend maker
Neat writer.

Louis Addy (11)
Castleford Park Junior Academy, Castleford

Game Day

As I hopped out of the car,
I knew I'd come from afar,
And I wouldn't be disappointed.
As my dad pointed at the stadium,
I took a deep breath of the buzzing and lively atmosphere around.
I heard a loud sound.
The fans were chanting and singing with passion,
As they were dressed in Arsenal shirts.
My favourite type of fashion.
I couldn't wait to see the Arsenal game.

Lucas Preda (12)
Chessington School, Chessington

Winter

W inter, winter is the best,
I play in the snow and get to rest.
N ights are short and full of joy,
T ime is vital, so enjoy.
E very time I try my best,
R emember it for the rest of your lives.

Chloe Watson (12)
Chessington School, Chessington

This Is Me

A feeling turns the body numb
N o feeling of fun
G reatness fades away
R eality slowly unveils
Y ou feel a great displeasure.

Ty Alleyne (13)
Chessington School, Chessington

Moss

A haiku

Small little zygote
Bryophytes are really old
From ripe sporophyte.

Tristan Padberg (13)
Chessington School, Chessington

This Is Me

Ingredients:
A cup of energy
A pinch of memory
A pound of passion
Some style and fashion
A litre of ambition
And lots of tradition
A spoon full of sugar
And a very good digger.

Instructions:
Firstly, slowly sift in your memory and passion
Stir in the energy and sugar till it's well stirred
Then add your confidence and passion too
For some liquid, add your ambition until it turns brown
Add a dash of tradition and fashion till it makes a sound
Pour your batter into the highest quality pan
Bake it in an oven until it smells divine.

Kim Do (11)
Collingwood School, Wallington

Things I Love

I'm a defensive warrior,
Dog lover,
Cat hater,
I'm a comedian,
My beautiful two dogs,
I'm as beautiful as a flower,
Exellent CDM in football,
Great gamer,
Excellent eater,
Oaktree hair,
Eyes like the ocean,
Brains like Albert Einstein,
Nerves nibbling at my stomach.

Dylan Anderson (11)
Coton-In-The-Elms CE Primary School, Coton-In-The-Elms

This Is Me

K etchup
A nt hater
D en maker
E lephant lover
N etball player.

J uice drinker
A dventurer
Y oga hater
E gg breaker like an egg hater.

Kaden-Jaye Bell (10)
Coton-In-The-Elms CE Primary School, Coton-In-The-Elms

This Is Me

My name is Jack
My friends are pretty wack
Sour and sweet
I live up on these streets
Friends are nice
In games, I roll the dice

Josh, he's happy
Sometimes I'm unhappy
I have an amazing family
The story ends happily
I love video games
People tell me I have a smart brain

Getting educated in school
Honestly, it's pretty cool
I have an adorable dog named Jess
She always makes a mess
I really love cake
Sometimes I get a stomach ache

When Jess makes a mess
I just have a rest
Logan is my best friend
I'm honestly starting to ascend
I really like football
Always liked meatballs
Getting help by Place 2 Be
This is me!

Jack Storey (11)
Easington Colliery Primary School, Easington Colliery

About Me

I'm funny and I'm happy,
I'm helpful and I'm kind,
I have not got a favourite colour,
As I just can't make up my mind.
I really love school, my teachers and my friends,
I like reading my stories right to the end,
I'm sporty, I'm friendly, I'm cheerful and I'm glad,
I really like spending time with my dad.
I'd eat pizza all day - I just can't stop,
Big strawberries too, with ice cream on top,
I'm silly, I'm jolly, I'm tricky and I'm wise,
My favourite food is a burger with big curly French fries.

Mia Lawler (11)
Easington Colliery Primary School, Easington Colliery

This Is Me

To make me you will need...
Half of a cup of sass
A whole jar of loyalty
Sprinkles of unkindness
A lot of jars of love
A few spoonfuls of laziness
A few jugs of creativity
Now just add the water

Firstly, add the spoon full of laziness
Secondly, the jugs of creativity
Thirdly, of course, add the jars of love
Then the unkindness
Then the loyalty
Last but not least, the sass
Mix! Mix! Mix!...

Amelia Veitch (11)
Easington Colliery Primary School, Easington Colliery

Just Me
A kennings poem

I am a...
Funny Xboxer
McDonald's eater
Book reader
Wasp fleer
Brown lover
Legendary striker
Pancake creator
Decent basketballer
Insane footballer
Tennis player
Good dodgeballer
Pizza maker
And finally...
Good person.

Luke Mathwin (10)
Easington Colliery Primary School, Easington Colliery

This Is The Real Me

I am kind,
I am happy,
I am calm,
And a little bit yappy,
But this is me and my personality,
I don't have enemies,
I only have frenemies,
This is me!

Kieran Mcgloen (11)
Easington Colliery Primary School, Easington Colliery

Me

M inecraft gaming is the best
A nd
Y ouTube ghost hunters are the best
S unshine is fun
O lympic games is fun
N ever ever be naughty

G riffin is a mythical creature
R eally funny
I 'm sometimes moody
F abulous fun
F riends always be kind to
I 'm a joker
N ever lie.

Mayson Griffin (8)
Elms Farm Primary School, Birmingham

Me!

S miles
A nd
M inecraft is the best
I 'm always grumpy
R eally fun

M agnificently talented
O mar is the worst
H ate vegetables
A nd
M unching pizza is the best
M oody all the time
A nd
D ecember is my favourite month.

Samir Mohammad (8)
Elms Farm Primary School, Birmingham

My Kindness Pledge

This is me
And it is my pledge to be
The best version of myself
That I can be
To see the light in the dark
And to be a little bit of light
In a bad situation.

I might just be ten
But I could change the
Course of the future.
I could be the next
Prime minister or I could
Be a marine biologist and
Discover new sea life. I
Will help everyone I can
Because it is not enough
To just be kind, you
Have to be kinder than
Is necessary.

I believe in
Doing things for people, kind
Things for people.
Not because
Of who they are or
What they can do for us
But because of who
You are or the person
You want to become.

This is me
Pledging to be
Kind, brave, and unapologetically me.

Keiva Bailey (10)
Featherstone Primary School, Erdington

This Is Me

T rying all the time
H appy when I am with my family
I love big, fluffy pandas
S uper loving and caring.

I love books
S ometimes I can be a nuisance.

M ostly I stay in bed (especially on the weekends)
E njoy coming to school.

Inayah Sheraz (11)
Featherstone Primary School, Erdington

How To Be Annoying

Since the day I was born,
I made it my goal to be annoying as possible.
It brings me joy to my heart
To know I was annoying from the start.
It came to me like destiny;
To rile my mum and dad you see.

Although it was hard
I still proceeded to
Be as irritating as needed.
My favourite ways to annoy
My family include moaning daily
And tidying terribly.
I love a mess wherever I go,
So they can follow me so.

But no matter how hard I try
I'll never be as annoying as that orange guy...

Donald Trump!

Archer Blaxall-Kimber (9)
Harvington CE First School, Harvington

I Am Edward

I am Edward. I am rather tall.

A favourite thing of mine is football
M y hair is dark blonde, my eyes are blue

E xploring maps is something I like to do
D aily reading is what I also like
W alking is fun, but not quite a hike
A lesson in Geography is what I like best
R eading a book, I always hope to find a quest
D iligent, kind, and a good footballer is what I strive to be.

Edward Dorrell (9)
Harvington CE First School, Harvington

This Is Me

I love to play
And also shout yay!
I love to play with my friends
Friendship never ends!
'Cause friendship means the world to me.
I can't imagine what this world would be
Without a friend close to me
I love to go swimming
And don't mind singing
My name is Emilie
And my friends think I'm silly!

Emilie Zidani (9)
Harvington CE First School, Harvington

This Is Different Things

H arrison is my name!
A nimal man is my dream job
R unning is my favourite sport
R eading makes my heart smarter
I ce cream makes my head freezing
S wimming is my favourite habit
O range ice cubes are delicious
N othing is better than delicious sweets.

Harrison Black (8)
Harvington CE First School, Harvington

Me

B rave
O ver excited
B old
B eautiful
Y oung

I am nice, brave and bold.
I help people when they get hurt.
I am sporty and I teach people to do sport.

Bobby Callins (8)
Harvington CE First School, Harvington

My Dog Teddy

T eddy loves dogs and toys
E verything he loves to lick
D oes what he's told to do
D igs in the mud too
Y oung Yorkshire terrier puppy.

Heidi Bishop (10)
Harvington CE First School, Harvington

Reflection

Both fire and ice,
I am a perfect mix of sugar and spice,

My name is Ummi!
I am ten years old,
I have a body of metal,
But a heart of gold

My family is my strength,
I love to do art,
My weakness is maths,
But I am very smart

My favourite colour is gold,
My favourite place is my school
I respect everyone,
And shine like a jewel

Keep me in your heart,
Not in your mind
I am Ummi!
One in a million kind.

Ummi Hoque (10)
Henry Green Primary School, Dagenham

Football Is The Best

F ootball helps release my stress,
O pen my mind,
O pen my brain,
T raining is the best way to be good.
B e like your best player,
A nd follow your dreams,
L ove to try new things,
L ove to be healthy.

Muhammed Bukera (10)
Leicester Islamic Academy, Leicester

All About Me And Pizza

Pizza is so yummy,
I can gulp it down my tummy,
It's super scrummy.

I don't get grumpy,
After it goes down my tummy,
It is so yummy.

In my tummy,
It is not at all scruffy,
All over the world, it is yummy in my tummy.

Aaminah Bukera (9)
Leicester Islamic Academy, Leicester

I Want To Be A Teacher

I want to be a...
A person who helps,
And doesn't say well,
Willing to sympathise for someone who's sad,
I'm very kind and caring,
But don't like yelling.
I will help you in the future.
I am a teacher.

Ayana Shakeel (9)
Leicester Islamic Academy, Leicester

This Is Me!

I like playing football,
But I hate every other sport.
I'll never step on a tennis court
Unless a football is brought
And winning is my only thought.

Awaab Hassan (10)
Leicester Islamic Academy, Leicester

Who Am I?

I am happy every day and everywhere.
I will share, even if they're ill.
And I am funny as a clown!
Finally, I am sharing as the earth.
I am Shahir.

Shahir Salman (9)
Leicester Islamic Academy, Leicester

This Is Me

On hard days
My heart is like a white ambulance
When my heart feels good
My heart is pink
Like a sticky lollipop
When my heart is calm
I feel blue like a summer sky
When my heart is purple
I feel full of beans
And I jump around.

Samantha Lorimer (7)
Leuchars Primary School, Leuchars

My Dreams

Sometimes I dream I'll wear purple jeans
Sometimes I dream I'll make it to big screens
Sometimes I dream I'll meet someone mean
Sometimes I dream I'll cry and I'll scream

Sometimes I dream I'll explode on the sun
Sometimes I dream I'll have some fun
Sometimes I dream I'll fly to the moon
Sometimes I dream I'll turn into a balloon

Sometimes I dream I'll eat my ice cream
Sometimes I dream that I'll meet the Queen
Sometimes my dreams get all scary
Sometimes I feel like a fairy

But all the things that my dreams are
Like the time I lived in our car
They always end up much better
Than the time I wore an itchy sweater!

Honor Porter Davison
Loretto Junior School, Musselburgh

I Want To Be

I want to be a dancer
That twirls just like a prancer,

I want to be a gymnast
That flips around really fast,

I want to be a ballerina
And twirl around in the arena,

I want to be a marine biologist
Who roams in the underwater forest,

I want to be a designer
That wears black eyeliner,

I want to be a vet
Who looks after everyone's pets,

I want to be a zookeeper
But that would make me a bad sleeper,

I want to be a conductor
Or just maybe a music instructor,

Which one should I pick?

Stella Jenkins
Loretto Junior School, Musselburgh

The Ups And Downs Of Life

When Covid started,
The downs,
Lonely and not connected
There are some ups,
Such as stronger bonds with my family
And homeschooling

My brother
The downs
Really annoying
Laughs when I get hurt
And the ups
Sometimes plays with me
Has glasses like me
Being just a bit taller than him

Being a horse lover,
The downs
Falling off
Being pushed into a barrow of horse manure

And the ups
Getting to hug them
Grooming them
Loving them

Having curly hair
The downs
Always tangly
Brushing it
And the ups
Getting it puffy
People saying how nice it is
Being in the 11% of people who have it.

Ellie Evans (11)
Loretto Junior School, Musselburgh

My Favourite Animals

My chickens are brown and white,
They can jump very high,
Like big brown kites.
My chickens are called Eggy and Paul
They look very big but are easy to haul

I love frogs,
They are cute and cool
And they live in little pools
I have a toy frog
And his name is Yibu
He lies in a bed
That is made of tissue

My hamster is very cute,
She doesn't make much noise,
It's like she is almost a mute
When I got her
She brought me great joy
Yet I didn't know
If she was a girl or a boy.

Alice Lockie (11)
Loretto Junior School, Musselburgh

When I'm Older

When I am older
I want to be an investor
Creating things at great pace
That will help to improve the human race

When I am older
I want to be an astronaut
But I wouldn't mind being a cosmonaut

I have a fear of planes
But I'm the one with all the brains

My favourite animal is a tiger
And I'm trying to become a better biker

Moving country was very hard,
But I made it without much regard,
Despite all those fears
I still shed no tears.

Xavier Jandrell
Loretto Junior School, Musselburgh

My Dog Lola

She's clever and super cute
But she'll still sometimes eat your boot

She's extremely funny
A bit like a bunny

She's super speedy
But not very greedy

Remember to keep her calm
Or she'll eat your lip balm

She's brown and white
And faster than light

She loves eating socks
And acts like a fox

She's simply a dog
Who might even eat your frog!

Oscar Borthwick (10)
Loretto Junior School, Musselburgh

This Is Me

I may be strange,
I may be weird,
I may be different,
I may have a weird eye,
But that's okay,
Because,
I am kind,
I am funny
I am loyal,
I am beautiful,
'Cause I am me,
And I love me,
Me is pretty great.

Sofia Legorburu (11)
Loretto Junior School, Musselburgh

This Is Me

My name is Jasmine and I like rhyming
To my nanna, who is the hero of the team
And I like eating cookie ice cream
My dream is to adopt a husky
All I want is my family
My dream job is the RSPCA
To help sick animals on their way
My favourite things are singing, drawing, huskies, friends and family
My birthday is the 24th of May
The season the sun comes out to play
My future is to have a house in the sky
So I can see my nanna, every day and night
My favourite colours are yellow and pink
All I want to do is be free like a bee
This is me.

Jasmine Leah Robinson (10)
Lower Kersal Community Primary School, Salford

This Is Me

A bbey is my best friend
L ove my family and friends
I like playing out
C ats are my favourite animal
I love eating chocolate
A ll I like is my phone

R ed is the worst colour
O range is the best colour
B rownies are my favourite food
I love my holidays
N ow what I like is to play chess
S ister, that's my role
O ne in a million, that's me
N ot just a sister, but a twin, that's me.

Alicia Grace Robinson (10)
Lower Kersal Community Primary School, Salford

Recipe Poem

To create me, you will need
A bit of intelligence
Some fun
Kindness
Games
Hot food
A lot of fruits
Speed

Now you need to
Sprinkle some fun and happiness
Stir and put in a cheesy pizza
Add a pinch of fun and a dash of brightness
Put in the oven for twenty minutes
After twenty minutes, take it out
Sprinkle some more fun and brightness.

Dario Ludwig (8)
Lower Kersal Community Primary School, Salford

Where Do I Come From?

I come from concrete buildings,
And family greetings,
Playing basketball with no light,
As the day turns to night,
The grind is a fight,
But the result is a delight.

I come from messing about with friends,
To seeing their brothers dying from skengs,
RIP, a funeral in their ends.

I come from indecisive weather:
Sun,
Rain,
Sun,
Thunder and lightning,
Grey clouds filling up the sky.
That doesn't bother me,
As I continue passing by,
Grinding to be something more,
Trying to enter the famous door,

It'll be a long journey I saw,
But I'm making it, that's what I swore.

I come from car meets,
And bikes in the streets,
Brand new BMXs,
Quick moving across the city,
This is the life we live,
Don't be playing,
We're nice, but we're just mistaken...

Gabe Simmonds (12)
Maplesden Noakes School, Great Buckland

My Life

I do and I love horse riding
Into the cross-country that's in a field
I like to hug them when I am sad
I do dressage and win every time
Brushing horses and making them clean
I teach them tricks
I do love jumping because it's fun
I love doing gymkhana
I go on family rides with my sister
I tidy my tack room and find myself
Hunting for my Matchy Matchy horse set
I gallop in fields and watch the sunset
Horse shows are the best.

Nevaeh (10)
Milton Abbot School, Tavistock

This Is Me

My favourite colour is green
You'll find me on screen
My friends play Fortnite
Some play it all night
I'm good at gaming, that's what I think
I have two dogs and one of them stinks.

Luca Dulare (10)
Nailsworth CE Primary School, Nailsworth

This Is Me Rap

I'm a...
Brave one,
A strong one,
A smart one.

I'm a...
Friendly,
Nice,
And a caring one.

My hobbies are...
Art,
Biking,
And fighting.

I love my...
Cats,
Dog,
Friends,
And family.

This is me.

Charlotte Harper (8)
Newtonmore Primary School, Newtonmore

All About Enis

E li is my sister,
N osy Eli,
I want a million pounds,
S neaky as a black panther,

H ot as lava,
A mazing Enis,
C appuccinos are my favourite,
I like jam roly-poly,
M y favourite seafood is anchovies,
U SA is where I want to go,
S kateboarding is my favourite,
A tlantis is my favourite.

Enis Hacimusa (8)
Normanhurst School, North Chingford

This Is Me

If I was the weather I would be a thunderstorm, because my brother is so annoying.
I would crackle until I would scare him.

This is me
My feelings make me different to everybody else.
My feelings are like waves sometimes little, big and medium.
My personality is respectful, full of it, kind, crazy, nuts, cheeky and funny.

This is me
I look like a nerd, with my mixture seaweed green eyes, and my tanned olive skin.
On the bridge of my button nose, I have Newcastle football glasses resting.

This is me
If I had a soul animal, I would be a panther because it is a majestic animal
We could ride into the distance and it is a really cool animal.

Aidan Blades (8)
Our Lady & St Peter RC Primary School, Bridlington

This Is Me

This is me
I have a strong body for being fit for football
I have long legs, for sprinting for the ball
I have brown shiny eyes like a tree trunk

This is me
I play football, a future football player for PSG
I dodge every football player easily like a master
I like playing video games like Horizon Forza 3 and FIFA 22
As well like playing basketball, throwing a fireball through the round iron hoop

This is me
I am a safe full of fresh, delicious chicken nuggets Ready to eat
And also a bowl full of yummy, cold ice cream.

This is me
I make a cheerful noise when I watch football
I do an angry sound when my naughty brother bothers me
And also do a sound saying pass! Pass! When I need the ball

This is me
I am a peaceful sun when I have peace
And also a raging tornado when I am mad

This is me
I have an athletic and fun heart
A peaceful and calm person
Also funny

This is me
A kind loving friend
I am loving
And peaceful.

Nikodem Biernat (9)
Our Lady & St Peter RC Primary School, Bridlington

This Is Me!

This is me,
My eyes are caramel-brown,
Ruffled brunette brown hair,
Always wearing a sporty red rugby kit,
Friendly, kind smile,
Brave, welcoming face

This is me,
My encouraging, thoughtful heart,
A hard-working, intelligent brain of a leader,
An uplifting, friendly, religious eight-year-old boy

This is me,
Athletic, rugby-loving boy,
The loyal captain of my rugby team
Always playing or training for super fantastic sports,
Making cool Lego cars in my free time,
Passionate, strong batter,

This is me,
My loud, kind voice always bellowing out jokes or encouragement,

My hilarious sarcastic jokes going on and on,
A fair, loyal, helpful friend, always sticking up for friends,
A hardworking but funny personality that puts everyone before myself.

Josh Miller (8)
Our Lady & St Peter RC Primary School, Bridlington

This Is Me

This is me
My eyes like a bright blue ocean in the sunrise
Slender long legs as long as a quarter of a football pitch.
As skilled as Neymar on the pitch, strong as metal, as fast as a cheetah.

This is me
Smell of a delicious lasagne fresh cooked
The nice smell of the pasta layer
All the crispy cheese layer at the top and also the nice meaty layer as well.

This is me
I'm as tempered as a lashing tornado
I'm as polite as the sun
I'm as kind as nature.

This is me
I am a sensei at dodgeball at dodging balls
Good at throwing and smashing the ball at the other team.

Nico Ferre (9)
Our Lady & St Peter RC Primary School, Bridlington

This Is Me

This is me
I am clever and brave and bossy.
I have gentle black hair like the dark sky at night.

This is me
I'm a raging tornado when I do a death run on Roblox.
My fast legs run as fast as a cheetah
When passing the ball to my teammates.

This is me
Melting cheese with a slice of pepperoni pizza ready to eat.

Jayson Celohorty (8)
Our Lady & St Peter RC Primary School, Bridlington

Who Is Freddy?

He is a brave, brilliant, bewitching, bright boxer
As strong as a giant, hungry tiger
As fast as a flying comet, soaring through space

If Freddy were a famous pro boxer he would be Tyson Fury!

He's game-playing
Goal-scoring
Boxing-loving
Football-starring

Who is Freddy?

It is me!

Freddy Derbyshire (9)
Our Lady of Perpetual Succour Primary School, Widnes

This Is Me

To create me you will need:
A room full of chaos,
A scoop of pick 'n' mix,
10 handfuls of anxiety,
5lbs of mischievous people,
1 slab of Burger King,
A sprinkle of excitement and love.

Now you will need to:
Add a scoop of pick 'n' mix.
Next, add your room full of chaos.
Mix until smooth while adding your 10 handfuls of anxiety.
When smooth, add in your 1 slab of Burger King.
As well, add in your 5lbs of mischievous people.
Add it all in a square tin as well, spread it.
Leave it in the oven for 20 minutes. Take it out.
Sprinkle the excitement and love onto it.

There you are, this is me!

Lily Woolmer
Phoenix St Peter Academy, Lowestoft

This Is Me

I mportant to my family.
M ummy is my favourite.
O sker is my sister's toy baby.
G reat and supportive.
E llie is my friend.
N ever give up.

R ose is my flower.
O liver is my friend.
S miggle is my favourite store.
E mily is my friend.

L una is my cat.
A pples are my favourite fruit.
P eyton is my friend.
P ineapples are the worst.
I sla is my BFF.
N ell is my favourite word.
G oats are my favourite animal.

Imogen Rose Lapping
Phoenix St Peter Academy, Lowestoft

This Is Me

E llie the cat sat on the mat.
L illy the lizard saw a gnat.
L an the dog went for a walk.
I sla is my friend and she can talk.
E veryone is funny so I must be funny.

F ryer loves chocolate cake and money.
E lliot sat on the mat.
L izzy saw a cat.
T oby loves to play.
O h and I love May.
N ippy loves to eat and I meet my friends.

Ellie Felton (7)
Phoenix St Peter Academy, Lowestoft

Basketball

B asketball is my favourite sport
A nkle-breaking shooting all day
S tealing the ball and scoring in game
K neeling down as I scrape the floor
E veryone shaking hands and sweating
T elling the other team, "GG"
B ack on round two, not giving up
A mazing gameplay on our team
L istening to them in rage
L eaping up and down as we just won.

Hadleigh Hitcham (9)
Phoenix St Peter Academy, Lowestoft

The Wonderful Land Of Dinosaurs

D inosaurs ruled the world!
I nside the cave the dinosaurs lay.
N egatively, as they eat each other.
O wning the land as they walk.
S tanding in the cold breeze as the little ones play.
A s they eat leaves off the autumn trees.
U nexpectedly jumping out of the water.
R oaming the world millions of years ago.

Lacie Lapping (9)
Phoenix St Peter Academy, Lowestoft

Me

D ogs are my favourite animal because they cuddle me.
E veryone wants to play with me.
M y favourite food is macaroni cheese.
P ixie is my big sister's name.
S wimming is my favourite sport.
E arly mornings are not for me.
Y ummy yummy, ice cream in my tummy.

Dempsey Dyer (8)
Phoenix St Peter Academy, Lowestoft

My Personality

K enzy is my name, I'm kind and love animals
E verybody says I'm full of surprises
N ever lets you down
Z oos are my favourite place to go
Y es, I am cheeky, but I'm very thoughtful too.

Kenzy Hoskin (9)
Phoenix St Peter Academy, Lowestoft

Space

S pace is amazing!
P lanets spin silently.
A mazing stars shine.
C limbing rockets fly through the sky.
E ating space food in my rocket.

Ronald Stanaitis (9)
Phoenix St Peter Academy, Lowestoft

My Amazing Dog, Rolo!

R idiculously handsome face.
O ut in my garden, being crazy.
L icking the wind, like a weirdo.
O bviously amazing, the best boy!

Evie Grist (10)
Phoenix St Peter Academy, Lowestoft

What I Love To Do

I love to feed my animals
With a smile on my face
Snake, beetle, stick are all my faves
When I have time I go to the beach
I play and say yippee!

Alexis-Grace Woolmer-Crosswell (9)
Phoenix St Peter Academy, Lowestoft

Things I Like!

I like dogs and tennis balls
I like chocolate and waffles.

I like doughnuts and lollipops
I like biscuits and bars.

I like Christmas
I like presents.

I like tea, I like school
I like rollerblades and I like you.

These are the things that I like
And I hope you like them too!

Darcy Orr (10)
Saints & Scholars Integrated Primary School, Armagh

Gengar

It is purple and round,
And has been crowned,
The ultimate Pokémon,
And I have drawn a picture.

Tyler White (9)
Saints & Scholars Integrated Primary School, Armagh

The Things That Make Me!

The key to make me

Add a bit of braveness
Why not sprinkle some kindness?
Mix some clever to make it better!
This is me!

It should turn blue
And it should smell a lot like shampoo
This is the recipe that makes me
This is me!

Shushil Varsani (10)
South Rise Primary School, London

This Is Me!

     J ust
yo **U** ur
     S imple
     T errific
     I ntelligent
     N atural person!

Justin Rwatangabo (10)
South Rise Primary School, London

Always Dancing

D ay by day, hour by hour
A ny place, any time
N ever giving up my passion for dancing
C ome, I will share my favourite hobby
E ven if I have to spend my time creating dances.

Ella Whitehorn (11)
St Anthony's Primary School, Spateston

Sam

Hey, I'm Sam
I've always cooked in a pan
I like watching TV shows
I manage patience no

I like football
Sometimes I can be at a mall
I love funny videos
I can listen to the radio

I have a sister
She can be annoying
I'm known as a mister
I love trampoline parks enjoying

I have multiple friends; Peter, Fiyin, the list goes on
Ife, Sooma, Harry, Larry, Alex, Ethan, Shanoy
and more
Morgan, Zac, Kengah and Theo, you get the gist
I have many friends, that never offends

I have good taste in editing
I need my crediting
I'm in year 6
I need some fix

I use CapCut
Editing in my hut
I love gaming
Roblox, Rocket League and Minecraft

Now you know facts about me
You might as well agree
I have a number of friends
And never ends.

Sam Falusi (11)
St Mary's Catholic Primary School, Tilbury

Identity Poem

Doing well on my test, because I want to be the best
I have a special pet, a secret area in my chest, there is no contest

Hot chocolate is my favourite, not much can beat it
A friendship more than a gift, a friendship that's fair with care

Alex is my name, friendship's my game
Everyone deserves a friend
But the world is in pain and war
Global warming, closer and closer
Animals are worse and in danger

Global warming is like a cookie in a cup of milk
We must remove the cookie from the milk
Before it crumbles, like how the earth will crumble
In the grasp of global warming

I am good at helping people when they are dejected
If we try our best in everything, we would be able to save our planet.

Alexandros Mistakidis (11)
St Mary's Catholic Primary School, Tilbury

Fabulous Fiyin

The world keeps turning
I keep growing
Sometimes I wonder what's going to happen
The world is filled with joy
And so am I

My name is Fiyin
I work hard
But sometimes I get lost
I live a life of hopes and dreams
Which I hope will come true

My brain is growing every day
But don't know what's stopping me from getting the goal
So now let's go back to the beginning

My name is Fiyin
The world keeps turning
I keep growing
Sometimes I wonder what's going to happen
The world is filled with joy
And so am I.

Fiyin Osinuga (11)
St Mary's Catholic Primary School, Tilbury

Why Me?

I love dogs
I hate cactuses and I hate frogs
Because they stick their tongue out at me
And I hate it
Why me?

Never bring me a cat
Or I'll splash it
That's a fact!
They always sharpen their claws
And try to scratch!
Why me?

Don't bring me orange juice
I only like apple juice
Why do I always get in trouble?
Why me?

I hate McDonald's paper straws
Why can't they have real plastic straws?
The paper straws always break!
This always happens to me
Why me?

Samuel Onafuye (9)
St Mary's Catholic Primary School, Tilbury

Who Am I If I Don't Have God On My Side?

I am a powerful girl with a strong personality
Who am I if I don't have God on my side?
I am supported to grow wisely and smart
With God always there for me

I reach goals to a high extent
Who am I if I don't have God on my side?
I am a smart child with comportable behaviour
As God has guided me to

I sometimes sin but overcome them
Who am I if I don't have God on my side?
Then I make sure I don't do the sin again
When God guides me to do the right things.

Sophia Chimereanyinma Ogu (9)
St Mary's Catholic Primary School, Tilbury

When I'm Older

When I'm older
What will I be?

Will I be an astronaut
Zooming through the stars
Staring at planets
And jumping on Mars?

Will I be a dentist
Fixing old teeth
Or be a rapper
Dropping down sick beats?

Will I be a YouTuber
Constantly editing
Drinking lots of coffee
And eating lots of toffee?

Nobody knows
What I will be
Soon we will know
In the future, we will see!

Tilly Fagbore (9)
St Mary's Catholic Primary School, Tilbury

This Is Me

I'm tender and mild
I live as a child
And my family drives me wild

My favourite animal is a monkey
Which makes me very lucky

I'm friendly to family
So I'm never, never lonely

My favourite food is jollof
And I love to have pofpof

I'll not go down
So don't make me frown.

Lisa Addo-Tenkorang (9)
St Mary's Catholic Primary School, Tilbury

Who Inspired Me In My Daily Life?

M y best teacher who helps me a lot in my learning
R espects me
S he is kind to everyone in the playground and in class

O nly smiles when she makes funny jokes
S he is very kind to other people
A lways makes me laugh and smile
S he smiles like the bright sun.

Ellie Beadle (11)
St Mary's Catholic Primary School, Tilbury

I'm Always Happy

I am a lovely person
I like to help people
I like Gamer Girl
I like to read and always sing beautiful songs

I love Little Mix songs
I love pink dresses
I like art and maths

I like gaming
I love swimming
I pray to Jesus to help me every day
I'm always happy.

Amarachi Oguledo (11)
St Mary's Catholic Primary School, Tilbury

All About Me

M olly, my bestie forever and ever
I 'll swell up in tears about cute puppies and dogs
R ose milk, one of my favourite drinks
I 'm engrossed in Blackpink music
A raging fire to my delight
M y amazing pet, my dog, Blackfire.

Miriam Digy (10)
St Mary's CE (VC) Primary School, Bridport

Together Is Me!

A sprint of happiness
Roblox there, Roblox here
Creativity everywhere
Writing coming, writing going
Family there, family up here
Together in me
Joy there, joy here
School standing, school teaching
Cousins playing, cousins leaving
Friends with me, friends with them
Swimming fun, swimming splash
All together in me!
Love there, love here
Doughnuts coming, doughnuts munching
Football winning, football losing
Albania big, Albania small
Nice here, nice there
Family everywhere
Together in me
Peace here, peace there
Siblings with me

Writing down, writing up
Games everywhere
Sports going, sports coming
All together in me.

Marsela Martini (10)
St Mary's RC Primary School, Clapham

Triumphant Thomas

Spelling, reading at home
And in school I fly through
If I read Through the night
I'll be tired, moody and miserable
If I'm in a football mood
I will score a Hat-trick Or two
Maybe if I score well in My test
I could have a treat
If I am good
I will get good things
And if I'm A drawer
So then a reader
And tomorrow a leader
Like the pattern in the poem.

Thomas Mushrafi (10)
St Mary's RC Primary School, Clapham

Zachary's Spectacular Personality

He puts his family first
Even when he is dying of thirst
More generous than the rest
Always tries his best
A smart, generous boy who knows his manners

Then comes his creativity
It is his favourite activity
He can definitely do art
But cannot throw a dart
A smart generous boy who knows his manners

Next come his friends
One of his best friends
Can swim to every deep end
That friend can also do a back bend
We will be friends till the end.

Zachary Harper-Simpson (11)
St Mary's RC Primary School, Clapham

My True Self

Jayden runs around on the ground
Playing in the snow
Taking chances, taking risks
He knows where to go
The cool breeze touches his face
His angelic voice makes his heart race
This is me
Showing who he is
Being what he wants
Ravens and eagles fly high
In the blue sky
As he grabs his magic wand
Shades of blue fly like fireworks
Oh Jayden is truly bright
His favourite moment of the day
Is night.

Jayden Gyamfi-Robinson (10)
St Mary's RC Primary School, Clapham

My Personality

I'm very creative
This is me
Full of joy and happiness
I express my emotions in my art
Sometimes I can be a shining star
But sometimes I feel like the puddle at the side of the path.

My favourite season is winter
Sometimes it gives me the shivers
When I take off my hat it's covered in snow
While the moonlight glows
My brown hazel eyes and my brown silky hair
Like the lights that glow in a funfair.

Megan Cadavid Monuz (10)
St Mary's RC Primary School, Clapham

Birthday

It's my birthday
People come to play
Before I was a little boy
Who played with big toys
I also love animals
But I am not a fan of them all
People come, people go
People eat, people stay neat
But it's my birthday
"Please may I stay"
"Here's a gift"
Said Uncle Tim
We are taking a train
Later I will explain
I only have one day
For my birthday.

Triomphe Peres (11)
St Mary's RC Primary School, Clapham

Me

Family and friends
Loves to play football, basketball,
Basically any games
Playing games here and there
Even PlayStation games
History, geography and maths
Are favourites for me
Football, hockey rules for me
Growing to be a footballer
Or a walker or a swimmer
I am proud to be me!

Tyrone Kwaako (11)
St Mary's RC Primary School, Clapham

Stefan's Life

I'm here, I'm there, I'm everywhere
Winning or losing
Swimming or playing
Football or basketball
Hopes and dreams
Non-favourites go to favourites
Friends or family
Teachers and assistants
Maths or English
And this is me.

Stefan Fernandes (11)
St Mary's RC Primary School, Clapham

About Me!

My name is Hawwa and my favourite food is pizza.
My age is eight and I love to learn new stuff,
Like how to count in my nine times table.
I love playing with my toys and putting them back
Really nicely and carefully.
I like to do art on Thursdays and Friday
With my paint and colours.
My favourite animal is a cat
Because they are soft and fluffy,
And a bird
Because they hum every time in the morning
And that is how I wake up.

Hawwa Zabar (8)
St Stephen's CE Primary School, Little Harwood

How To Create A Darcie Diva

Hi, my name is Darcie, can't you see
D-A-R-C-I and E
I've got curly hair and pretty clean feet
I hope y'all enjoy my really sick beat...
I've had enough of school and I really need a break
I would rather be in the pool or eat a cupcake
I just wanna chill, just me and my gang
We don't need the thrill, we just like to hang
I like the outdoors, I like wearing my shades
And I'll keep them on until the sun fades
Big hair, don't care, big hair, don't care
Big hair, don't care!
I'm back again with some really sick rhymes
You think yours is good, well listen to mine
You might think you have a really great song
Well guess what, it sounded all wrong!
You need to work on your childish rap
I'm gonna whip you up like a chocolate frap!

I like happiness and going in the pool
I could roast you all day, yes even in school
It takes style and grace to rap like this...
I have a lot of talent that you don't wanna miss!
Big hair, don't care, big hair, don't care
Big hair, don't care!
I can play piano and that's really sick
It's because I like music
Jazz is my passion
And I play saxophone in a real cool fashion
Yeah, you heard me right
It takes style and grace to rap like this...
I have a lot of talent that you don't wanna miss!

Darcie Morris (10)
The King's School, Macclesfield

What Makes Me Me

Hello, my name is Max,
Quite a young chap,
I am ten, so is Ben,
We both like cars,
And sweets in jars,
I like F1 but that's not for Tom,
I like Harry Potter, he thinks that's hotter,
Charlie's my pal, I met him at school,
We have fun, he's really cool,
There's also James Heald,
We like to play on the field,
And there's Matthew too,
To mention but a few,
I like to run, but it gets me muddy,
I do it with Jack, my buddy,
I would go on, my friends list is long,
Diego, Matteo and so on and so on...
This poem is about me,
But as you will see,
Without my friends, who would I be?

Max Westwood (10)
The King's School, Macclesfield

Sef Is My Name

Sef is my name,
Snooker is the game
And I'm when older I wish for fame.

Chess is what I love to play,
Funny things are what I love to say
And I hate it when the clouds turn grey.

Reading's what I love to do,
And playing video games too.
So my favourite animal at the zoo
Is the crocodile, yes, that's true.

I'd like to know who you wanna be,
But so far, this is me.

Sef Cooper (11)
The King's School, Macclesfield

This Is Me

A wesome is me.
R esilience is my strength.
I maginative with my writing I am.
Y earning for learning.
A dept as Einstein.
N ever say you can't as everything is possible.

N ever give up.
A lways try your best,
S upport others.
S uccess is my goal.
A im sky-high.
B elieve in yourself.

Ariyan Nassab (10)
The King's School, Macclesfield

This Is Me!

Hey, my name is Will
And I've got lots of skills
I am as fast as a cheetah
And I'm as kind as a cat
But sometimes, I can be...
As sneaky as a rat!
I love everything about football
And when my friends and I play
We give it our all!
I have blue eyes
I have silky, soft, straight hair
I love my food
And my favourite fruit is pear.

William Wallace (8)
The King's School, Macclesfield

The Life Of A Hutchins

I'm a massive City fan,
Around the ground I ran.
A solid centre-back,
No need to attack.
I can't stop chatting,
I criticise England's batting.
I ain't the tallest,
And not the fastest.
With a great sense of humour,
Not one to spread a rumour.
I'm really sporty,
With my parents over forty.

This is me.

Jack Hutchins (11)
The King's School, Macclesfield

About Me

Violins make me dance while thrifting's good to glance,
Sydney's my home, it's where I'm not alone,
History and mysteries make me joyful when there's victory,
Sushi makes me groovy, so do happy movies,
I love koala bears and some tasty pears,
But my family and friends will definitely last and never end.

Ella Collins-Webb (11)
The King's School, Macclesfield

This Is Me!

Yo! I'm a pinch of kindness mixed with mood
Xbox is my home
Warzone on its own
City is my club
Etihad all the way home.

Drip is what I'm known for
Supreme is my middle name
I love my family like I love Little Moons
My sisters act like wild baboons!

William Johnson (10)
The King's School, Macclesfield

J2 Charlie

Hello, my name is Charlie
Selhurst is my home
Supporting Palace everywhere I roam
I am a bit naughty, you can't say you're not
Knee-sliding around the Astro
I'm definitely not an angel, I've not got a halo.

Charlie Kay (11)
The King's School, Macclesfield

Freddie

F is for Freddie, as free as a fox.
R is for rugged, as rugged as rocks.
E is for energy, like a jack-in-the-box.
D is for dynamic, as strong as an ox.

Freddie Robinson-Pickles (8)
The King's School, Macclesfield

My World

When I grow up I want everything to change.
I want zoos to turn into wildlife sanctuaries,
I want people of every colour to grow up and get an education,
I want children to be free to do what they want,
Not what everyone else wants,
I want kids to be kids instead of slaves,
I want pride month to be celebrated far and wide,
The rainbow flag to be soaring high and the people not to hide,
I want to stop bullying and genocide,
I want as much attention to kids' mental health as body health,
I want to change the world for my sister's sake because her mental health is at stake.
But no, of course, I can't change the world.
In fact, the world is against me.
I am a kid, I am a girl,
So I start to think of an imaginary world,
But sadly it's in my head.
Oh, the world would change if they just let kids decide instead.

Ava Stephenson-Hyde
The Shade Primary School, Soham

My Life

C uddling Pickles the cat
H aving fun on Spook
A nd playing with friends
R unning from monsters in Minecraft
L earning to swim
I love football
E ating strawberries.

Charlie Mardon
The Thomas Coram CE School, Berkhamsted

Just Me

Although I'm as sleepy as a cat
I'm as adventurous as a rat
I adore cuddling into blankets
But I love to tinker around with trinkets

My eyes are as grey as a rainy day
But a screen makes me play
A fountain of chocolate drips down my head
The sight of dark chocolate fills me with dread

The sight of the slithering Northern Lights
Just erupts me with delight
I stop what I'm doing when I see snow
When I'm asked to come back in - No!

Science and writing make me so true
But the idea of addition fills me with blue
I love to read lots of books
And I don't care about looks

I'm just me.

Taparni Delamere (11)
Tweedmouth Community Middle School, Spittal

All Of Me

Bossy as a queen bee
Being creative is me
Those legs that sprint at netball
Although sometimes I may fall

I'm as sassy as a snake
I like to eat chocolate cake
I'm as determined as a cat
Trying to catch a rat

My hair is plain brown, though
I wear an imaginary crown
I think I'm the queen
And I love ice cream

As lazy as a sloth, I am
And as clumsy as an ostrich
I like turquoise, purple and pink
You'll see me in one blink

My dog is loyal
So am I
My friends are kind

So am I
My family is loving
So am I

I am me
Just me
Only me
All of me.

Sadie Gregory (11)
Tweedmouth Community Middle School, Spittal

This Is Me

This is me
As busy as a bee
As happy as can be
As lazy as a sloth
As crazy as can be

I am as adventurous as a butterfly
As kind as a dog
I like pigs in blankets
And little cute frogs

I am as shy as a mouse
Like an excited bunny
I bounce
Brave like a lion
But don't worry, I won't pounce.

Isla Stewart (10)
Tweedmouth Community Middle School, Spittal

This Is Me

I support Liverpool
I live in Berwick-Upon-Tweed
I read books
I play Pet Simulator X
I play football
I like football
I play Apex Legends
I play Fortnite
I like snakes
I eat sweets
I have a computer
And last thing,
I don't like Arsenal.

Layton Reap (10)
Tweedmouth Community Middle School, Spittal

My Life And Feelings

I'm helpful to my mum
I'm courageous
When the sun is out, I feel as happy as a rainbow
When I'm with my family, I feel over the moon
The moon shines brighter than the sun
I love everyone and everything
I feel the smartest of them all
The world is my canvas and I am the paintbrush
I love the world more than anything
Me and my friends are really good mates
Love is really important
Respect everyone, every day
Save animals
Love animals, even if they aren't cute
I'm passionate about fashion and art.

Grace Emma Howson (8)
Wakefield Methodist Junior & Infant School, Thornes

All About Me

My name is Bella, my favourite princess is Cinderella
Sometimes, people call me Karate Beam
Because sometimes, I lose my steam

My favourite animals are dogs, which carry logs
I want to work for the police, to help make peace

My favourite spread is jam, but I can't stand ham
I like to be on the net, and I really want a speed jet

My favourite subject is maths because it makes me laugh
I hope that this poem
Has revealed who I am
And knowing this will make you a fan!

Bella Reid (9)
Wakefield Methodist Junior & Infant School, Thornes

Me

My name is Betsy
I love to play football
Except when I fall
Then I don't like it at all

I like grapes
But definitely not crepes

I love to go to my grandma's
She's actually got the cars

I've got a sister called Bella
Who really likes Nutella.

Betsy Reid (9)
Wakefield Methodist Junior & Infant School, Thornes

Belle The Copy Of Ed Sheeran

Hello, my name is Belle
I have red-hot hair
I may look like a singer, it's probably Ed Sheeran
You may know him as a ginger, I look like a copy of him
The only thing is that I am short and I can't sing
I can only draw and play video games
I really want to change my name, but this isn't a game
I have long hair, not short,
It's as long as Rapunzel's hair,
It always gets called beautiful
And I don't know why
I am a copy of Ed Sheeran.

Belle Downey (10)
Wallsend Jubilee Primary School, Wallsend

This Is Me
A kennings poem

A pizza muncher
A cat befriender
A McDonald's lover
An animal keeper
A master gamer
A Roblox player
A lazy sleeper
A teddy cuddler
A sweet snatcher
An axolotl carer.

Olivia Carroll (7)
Westgarth Primary School, Marske-By-Sea

Mac And Cheese

M agnificent
A mazing
C heese

A bsolutely good
N ever goes to waste
D o try mac and cheese

C heese is the best
H ave all the time
E xcellent
E at always
S o much cheese
E at more.

Liam David (10)
Westlea Primary School, Westlea

Who Am I?

My eyes are sparkly nature green
My hair is a collage of golden brown
I would stumble just to see any scene
My heart can never make up its mind
I'm as chilled as a warm, cosy hammock
Sometimes I'm rude, sometimes I'm kind
Who am I?

Answer: Libby Matter.

Libby Matter (11)
Westlea Primary School, Westlea

Kerem

K ind and helpful to those who need help
E ating is fun
R ubik's cubes make you smarter
E arth protecting the climate and stopping deforestation
M y friends and family are helpful.

Kerem (10)
Westlea Primary School, Westlea

My Favourite Sport

Hi, I'm Oliver
I really like volleyball
I am very good
This is me

    O bservant
    L ikeable
    I ndependent
    V ersatile
    E nergetic
    R eliable.

Oliver Gardner (11)
Westlea Primary School, Westlea

Family

F unny
A lot of laughing
M y family always help me
I like to play games with my family
L ove
Y ummy food to eat together.

Elissia Doka (10)
Westlea Primary School, Westlea

This Is Me

My eyes are as black as the void
My heart is as red as a flame
My hair as curly as an elephant's trunk
My voice is as loud as a hyena howling
This is me.

Shawn Rodrigues (10)
Westlea Primary School, Westlea

I Am Jackson

I am as tall as a board.
I am as awesome as a chimpanzee.
I am as smart as a scientist.
I like wading in water.
I like the creaking woods.
I like crunching food.
I am Jackson.

Jackson Hall (8)
Wildridings Primary School, Netherton

This Is Me

I am as friendly as a firework.
I am as cold as ice.
I am a kind kickboxer.
I like mixed maths.
I like proper pizza.
I like fierce fireworks.
I am Grace!

Grace Townsend (7)
Wildridings Primary School, Netherton

All About Me

I am as active as activities.
I am as helpful as a hamster.
I am as fun as a funfair.
I like bunny board games.
I like teddy bear toys.
I like monkey moves.

Xiyuan Ju (8)
Wildridings Primary School, Netherton

I Am Matas

I am better than Lebron James.
I am as small as an angry ant.
I am a lazy boy.
I like video games.
I like crunchy candy.
I like geography.

Matas Gecevicius (8)
Wildridings Primary School, Netherton

This Is Me

I used to be as lonely as one cloud in the sky,
But my friends had my back and I was able to fly.

Me and my friends are sometimes like in a movie scene,
When two fighters need to make up for something
And then realise that sometimes we do break up
But we will always make up.

My glasses are as blue as the sky,
And my heart is as white and fluffy as a marshmallow,
And can easily melt into an icky, sticky mess.
My wish is to go far with my horse riding because
It is the only thing that makes me feel as free as the wind.
I know my friends will be by my side forever
And they will always make me who I am.
So... this is me.

Phoebe Hinks (10)
Windmill Hill Academy, Windmill Hill

YOUNG WRITERS INFORMATION

We hope you have enjoyed reading this book – and that you will continue to in the coming years.

If you're the parent or family member of an enthusiastic poet or story writer, do visit our website **www.youngwriters.co.uk/subscribe** and sign up to receive news, competitions, writing challenges and tips, activities and much, much more! There's lots to keep budding writers motivated!

If you would like to order further copies of this book, or any of our other titles, then please give us a call or order via your online account.

Young Writers
Remus House
Coltsfoot Drive
Peterborough
PE2 9BF
(01733) 890066
info@youngwriters.co.uk

Join in the conversation!
Tips, news, giveaways and much more!

 YoungWritersUK    YoungWritersCW    youngwriterscw